CONNECTING CULTURES

CANADA - JAPAN

by John Stephen Knodell

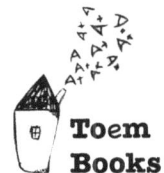

Toem
Books

Connecting Cultures: Japan & Canada

ISBN - 978-4-908152-00-9

Executive editor: Kirk Fernandes

Photo Credits
Newfoundland - David P. Lewis / Shutterstock.com p. 52
Remembrance soldier - meunierd / Shutterstock.com p. 62
Ice hotel - Marie Havens / Shutterstock.com p. 70

Toem Books
Tel. 011-839-3771
Email. info@to-em.com
札幌市中央区北２条西２６丁目２番１８号　２６WESTビル　4F　Room A

www.to-em.com

Dedicated to the Hokkaido Canada Society

TABLE OF CONTENTS

How to Use the Book

Connecting Cultures is a content-based English language textbook. It uses readings as the vehicle to help students learn and practice new vocabulary, conversational skills, useful grammar and more. Connecting Cultures focuses on Canadian topics of interest to Japanese students.

All of the readings contain grammar forms and vocabulary that are studied and practiced throughout each unit. This is done to enhance noticing of the grammar forms, and to show students how they are used in authentic situations. Within each unit, students are given tasks that focus on a particular linguistic objective. For example, unit one focuses on ways to give advice to people. Within the reading, students read about the life of Anne of Green Gables. She is a character full of life and who faces many problems in her life. Students look at the problems she had, and can give advice to her using practiced grammar forms.

If context is king, then teachers must assess what it is that their students need and want to learn, and adjust course content accordingly. This textbook was written to foster genuine interest, improve motivation, create opportunities for feedback, and use students' past experiences and knowledge to complete the tasks and activities for each unit.

Connecting Cultures Canada - Japan demonstrates the strong connection between these 2 countries, but can be used by any teachers interested in using a content-based approach to teaching English from the perspective of Japanese students and their interests.

About the Author

John Stephen Knodell has been an ESL/EFL teacher for over 20 years. He has taught at colleges in South Korea, and ran a language school in Montreal, Canada, for ten years. He has an M.Ed. from Calgary University, and degrees in TESOL and English Literature. He has taught English to a wide range of students, and continues to work as an English language lecturer at a university in Sapporo, Japan.

Unit Title	Vocabulary	Grammar Form
1 *Anne of Green Gables*	orphan, laugh at, charm, published, translated, rebuild, grow up, organization, survive	VERBS
2 *Bears in Canada*	usually, almost always, common, alone, seal, female, full of, afraid of, attack, weigh, hibernate	ADVERBS OF FREQUENCY
3 *The Arctic*	divided into, areas, native people, frozen, melts, covers, seals, arctic fox, spectacular, sleep well, igloos	ADJECTIVES
4 *Canada's Only Desert*	dry, temperature, rare, border, cactus, owl, rides his horse, grapes, rattlesnakes, farmers	PREPOSITIONS OF PLACE
5 *Canada's van Gogh*	not as famous as, mysteriously, paint, nature, forests, sick, quit his job, canoe	QUANTIFIERS
6 *Money*	baseball, antique, especially, valuable, bills, collect, hobby, quit, nobody, rare, check, worth	MAKING HOW QUESTIONS
7 *Religion*	disappear, traditions, greedy, suffer, temple, worried, monk, outside, servant, homeless, meditate	USING SAY / TELL / ASK / SPEAK
8 *Halifax Explosion, 1917*	caught fire, TNT, put out the fire, port, hit, each other, explosion, bombs, shore, didn't understand, burn	USING THERE IS / IT IS
9 *The Titanic*	embarrassed, sailor, skilled at, luxurious, sank, survive, tried to, lifeboat, coward, passenger, iceberg	HELPING VERBS
10 *Japanese People in Canada*	immigrate, several, made up his mind, move to, returned, weak, burned down, lonely, desire, named after	USING MADE
11 *Newfoundland*	similar to, continent, cod, seal, flipper, nickname, crickets, skunks, deer, porcupines, moose, float	STATIVE VERBS
12 *Winnie the Pooh*	veterinarian, take care of, cub, called it, donated, adventures, a wood, at that time,	IRREGULAR VERBS
13 *Remembrance Day*	soldiers, dangerous, remember, fought for, ended, protect, grow, buy, wear, silent, conflicts	TIME EXPRESSIONS
14 *Wish You a Merry Christmas*	celebrate, differences, fake, donate, turkey, churches, filled with, during, probably, open gifts	INFINITIVE VERBS
15 *Winter Activities*	activities, extremely, festivals, unusual, even, pond, rinks, stove, thousands of, charity, carnivals	USING GO __ ING
16 *Multicultural Country*	permanently, move to, immigrants, overcrowded, miners, agreed, degrees, compared to, foreigners	USING IF

This map of Canada will help students who don't know about Canada very well. When students read about Anne of Green Gables and Canada's smallest province, P.E.I., or want to know where Newfoundland is, or wonder where the real Winnie the Pooh grew up, this map can help them see where the stories take place.

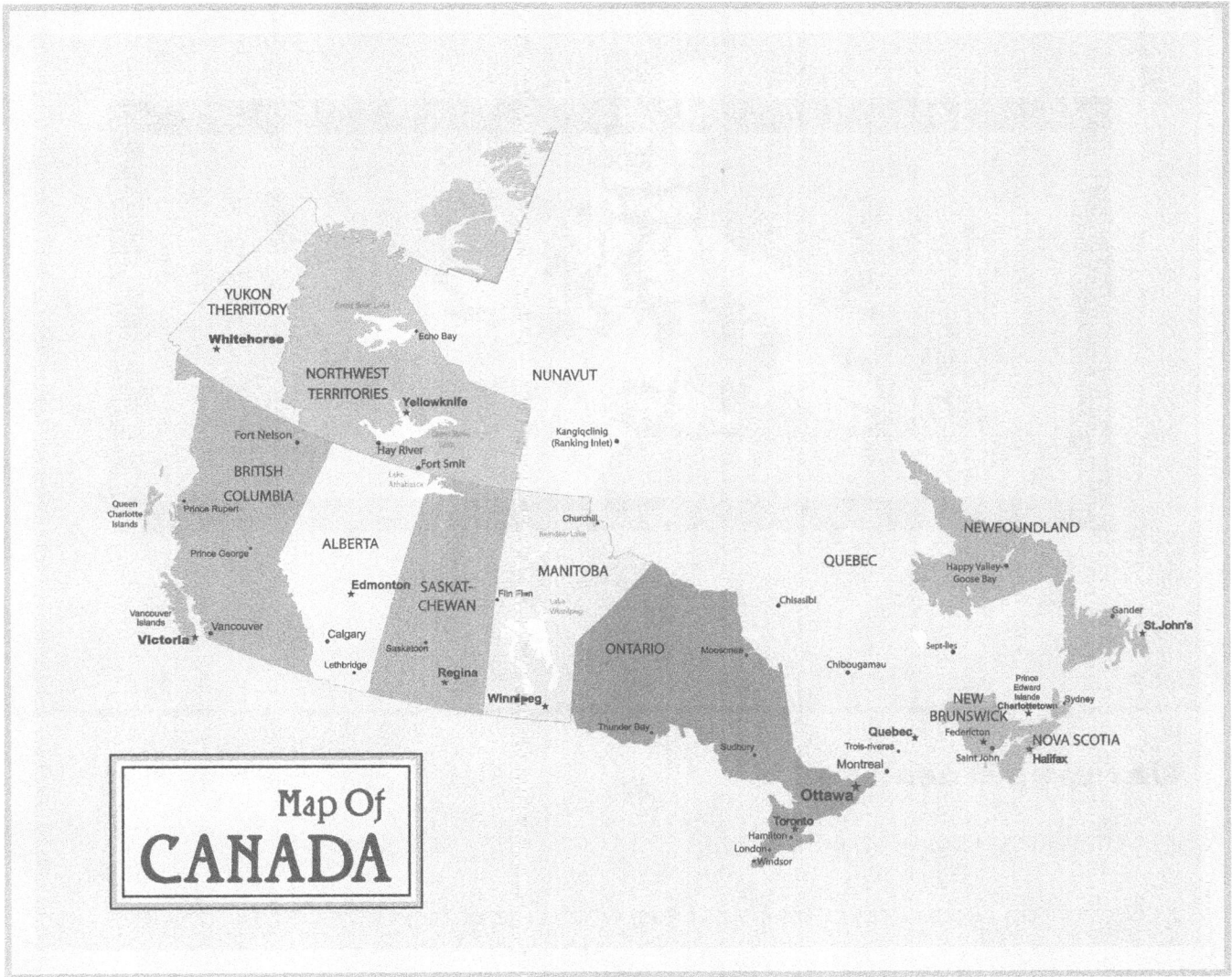

Unit 1

Anne of Green Gables

Warm-up Questions

1. What do you know about Canada?

2. Would you like to live on a farm? If yes, what kind of farm?

3. Have you ever
   - dyed your hair?
   - read Anne of Green Gables?
   - eaten Canadian food?

4. How was life different in the 1950s?

5. Anne had some enemies (敵) growing up. Did you have any enemies?

VOCABULARY

Write the correct word for the pictures below.

Orphan, laugh at, charm, published, translated, rebuild, grow up, organization, survive

1. _____ 2. _____ 3. _____ 4. _____ 5. _____

Anne of Green Gables

L. M. Montgomery wrote Anne of Green Gables in the early 1900s. It is a story about an orphan girl who grows up in Prince Edward Island (P.E.I.).

She has many difficulties in her life, but she survives them all. Her story teaches us to enjoy life, love our friends and family, and to be happy to be alive, even when life is hard. Maybe this is why Anne became popular in Japan.

Anne of Green Gables was published in Japan in 1952, and was translated by Hanako Muraoka. Hanako Muraoka had a Canadian friend named Miss Shaw. When Miss Shaw returned to Canada around 1940, she gave Hanako Muraoka a goodbye gift: Anne of Green Gables. Secretly, Hanako Muraoka translated the book, and after it was published, it became very popular. Many students read this story in high school all over Japan.

After WWII, life was not easy in Japan. Rebuilding the country was difficult. The story of Anne teaches people how to be happy even when life is hard And Anne had many difficulties in her life.

Anne has no family before she meets Matthew and Marilla. They are brother and sister, and they own a farm in P.E.I. Her first problem is that Marilla doesn't want to keep Anne.

Matthew and Marilla wanted to adopt a boy, not a girl. But Anne has a lot of charm, and the brother and sister decide to keep her. At school, Anne's classmates laugh at her hair and her big words, but she always tries to enjoy life.

Anne makes many mistakes in her life, but she tries very hard not to make the same mistake twice. As Anne says, "I make so many mistakes. But then just think of all the mistakes I don't make."

Anne's story ends when Matthew dies. Anne is away studying, but decides to go back home to help Marilla on the farm. To Anne, her family was the most important thing in her life.

Many Japanese tourists visit P.E.I. every year to see where Anne lived and had her adventures. Even Imperial Highness Princess Takamado helps the L.M. Montgomery organization, and maybe, she is also a fan of Anne's.

1 Understanding the Story

Answer the following questions.

1. When was Anne of Green Gables written?

   _____

2. How did Hanako Muraoka get the Anne of Green Gables book?

   _____

3. Why did Anne's classmates laugh at her?

   _____

4. What does it mean, "I make so many mistakes. But then just think of all the mistakes I don't make"?

   A) Making mistakes is bad   B) Always try hard   C) Don't worry too much about mistakes

5. What is very important in Anne's life?

   _____

2 Let's Practice...Giving Advice

Exercise 1: Read the sentences and circle the correct letter for the answer.

1. [It's raining] I think you _____ bring your umbrella.
   a) can   b) should   c) might

2. [She is very tired] Why _____ you rest.
   a) don't   b) mustn't   c) won't

3. [She caught a cold] It _____ be good if you stayed in bed.
   a) could   b) should   c) might

4. [He can't do his homework] You _____ ask your teacher more questions.
   a) won't   b) ought to   c) had to

5. [She lost her wallet] Maybe you _____ call the police.
   a) must   b) should   c) are able to

Exercise 2: Use these different ways to give Anne advice. Write your advice in the space below. Number 1 is already done, but give another answer. Be ready to give your advice in class.

1.	I think she should...	4.	Why doesn't she...
2.	If I were her, I would...	5.	It might be good if she...
3.	She could try...	6.	Maybe she should...

1. Anne talks too much (i.e. <u>I think she should listen more</u>)
2. Anne doesn't like her hair colour
3. Anne gets angry fast
4. Anne can't cook well
5. Anne jumps onto a sleeping old lady in her bed
6. Anne's family loses all of their money

1. _____

   _____

2. _____

   _____

3. _____

   _____

4. _____

   _____

5. _____

   _____

6. _____

   _____

3   Grammar Practice : Verbs

Here are some of the verbs used in the Anne of Green Gables story.

grow up, survive, teach, enjoy, become, return, translate,
meet, own, keep, decide, try, die, help, see

Finish the sentences below using verbs from the list on this page. Read the sentences carefully, and use the correct verb tense (past, present or future).

1. Anne _____ meeting her friends. She liked them very much.

2. My friend doesn't _____ a car. She walks to work every day.

3. In a desert, plants _____ even though (たとえ) there isn't a lot of water.

4. The bear, Winnie, did not _____ to Canada. It stayed in England forever.

5. Some people _____ their money under their beds.

6. When I was young, my grandmother _____ me how to tie my shoes.

7. Yesterday, Yumi _____ her friend at a museum.

8. In the future, maybe you _____ this book into Japanese.

9. Tomorrow, I might need your _____. Are you free?

10. Manzo Nagano _____ in Japan, but moved to Canada in 1877.

11. On the Titanic, many people _____ to get off the boat, but they didn't.

12. Two days ago, I _____ a movie about a painter who lived in a desert.

13. The painter _____ to live alone because she wanted to have a quiet life.

14. The painter _____ famous after she died.

15. All people _____. This is a fact of life.

4   Writing : Translation

Step 1: Look at the lyrics below for the theme song from Anne of Green Gables, and fill in the missing verbs.

きこえるかしら

きこえるかしら
ひずめの音
ゆるやかな丘をぬって
かけてくる馬車
むかえにくるの
むかえにくるのね
誰かが　わたしを
つれてゆくのね
白い花の道へ

風のふるさとへ
つれてゆくのね
つれてゆくのね

Can you _____ a horse _____ through a gentle hill?

A horse carriage _____ towards us

They are coming to _____ us

They must _____ coming to see us

Somebody _____ me to the avenue of white flowers

Hometown of the wind

They are _____ me

They _____ taking me

Step 2: Here is a list of the verbs used in the song. Write the past tense of these verbs, and what they mean in Japanese?

English Verb	Past Tense	Present Tense in Japanese
1. Come	1. Came	1. 来る
2. Hear	2. _____	2. _____
3. Run	3. _____	3. _____
4. See	4. _____	4. _____
5. Take	5. _____	5. _____
6. Burn	6. _____	6. _____
7. Be	7. _____	7. _____

Unit 2

Bears in Canada

Warm-up Questions

1. Do any wild animals live close to your home?

2. What do you always do in winter?

3. Are you afraid of any animals?

4. What do you think about zoos?

5. What do you think about hunting?

VOCABULARY

Write the correct words in the box below.

Usually, almost always, common, alone, seal, full of, afraid of, attack, weigh, hibernate

Vocabulary Quiz : Use the correct word to finish the sentences.

1. I don't like dogs. I am _____ dogs.

2. I _____ about 80kg.

3. My home is _____toys.

4. Be careful in that city. Bad men sometimes _____ people.

5. My dog is a boy. He is not a _____.

Bears in Canada

Canada is a land full of nature. People can see many kinds of animals in cities and outside cities. But one animal people *usually* don't want to meet is a bear.

It is the largest animal in Canada, and there are 3 different kinds of bears living across the country: the black bear, the grizzly bear, and the polar bear. Black bears are very common in Canada. They are smaller than grizzly and polar bears, but they are still very big.

In Canada, there are about 25 000 grizzly bears. They are around 2.5 meters tall, and weigh about the same as a small car. They usually live alone.

Every year, female grizzly bears have 1-4 baby bears. Grizzlies like to eat berries, but they love salmon. Before winter, grizzlies eat a lot of food every day (about 40kg).

Grizzly and black bears *almost always* hibernate in winter. They can sleep from 5 to 7 months. When they sleep, they never go to the bathroom. Polar bears don't hibernate in winter. They are active all year long.

Polar bears live in the north, around the Arctic Ocean. It is the largest bear in the world, and can weigh up to (以下) 550 kg. There are no berries or plants in the Arctic, so polar bears eat seafood, and their favourite is seal.

When a female polar bear has a baby, the baby weighs about .6kg. Many mothers build a home in the snow for their new family. Some of the homes have 2 or 3 rooms.

The Arctic is full of ice in winter. This helps polar bears catch their food. In summer, polar bears have to go on land. They occasionally go into towns because they are hungry. The people in the towns are afraid of the bears.

All bears rarely attack people. If you meet a bear, the bear will usually walk away from you. Black bears often keep their babies in trees, and they won't attack people if they get close to their babies.

Grizzly mothers are different. They sometimes attack people if they get close to their babies. Most attacks by grizzlies are done by mother grizzlies.

1 Understanding the Story

Circle the right letter for the questions below. Answers for questions 4 & 5 aren't in the story.

1. Polar bears _____ sleep for a long time (hibernate) in winter.
       a) often   b) never   c) always

2. Grizzly bears _____ attack people if people are close to their babies.
       a) never   b) occasionally   c) (nothing)

3. The biggest bear ever found was a _____ bear.
       a) grizzly   b) polar   c) black

4. People walking in forests should always carry _____.
       a) a gun   b) pepper spray   c) a bear costume

5. People should never _____.
       a) feed a bear   b) take a bear's picture   c) fight a bear

2 Let's Practice...Routines

The words below are called Adverbs of Frequency. They help explain how often something happens. In a sentence, they can go in many places:

Always - 100%	Occasionally - 25-75%
Almost always - 98%	Seldom - 5-10%
Usually - 90%	Rarely - 1-10%
Often - 80%	Almost never - 1%
Sometimes - 25-75%	Never - 0%

ヒント

I usually drink coffee for breakfast.
Sometimes, I watch TV at night.

She is always early for class.
They are rarely noisy.

Answer these questions using the Adverbs of Frequency above.

1. What time do you usually wake up in the morning?

_____

2. How often do you eat lunch at a restaurant?

_____

3. What do you sometimes do in the afternoon?

_____

4. What do you never bring to this class?

_____

5. When do you do your homework?

_____

6. Who never comes to class late?

_____

7. Where do you almost never go?

_____

8. What do you rarely drink?

_____

3   Writing: What's Your Routine

Write a short description of what you do during the day. First, pick a day. And then, explain your morning, afternoon, and night routine.

In the morning, I always _____, but I never

_____. Sometimes I wake up at _____. After I

wake up, I usually _____. I _____ watch TV

in the morning, and I _____ brush my teeth.

In the afternoon, I often _____, and I always

_____. If the weather is nice, I usually _____.

At night, I occasionally _____, but I never

_____. I usually sleep at _____.

17

Unit 3

The Arctic

Warm-up Questions

1. What do you think about cold weather?

2. Where is the coldest (寒い) place in your country?

3. Would you like to visit the Arctic? Why or why not?

4. How is the weather where you live?

5. Do you do anything to help the environment (環境)?

VOCABULARY

Write the correct word for the pictures below.

Divided into, areas, native people, frozen, melts, covers, seals, fox, spectacular, igloo

1. _____ 2. _____ 3. _____ 4. _____ 5. _____

The Arctic

The Arctic is a very cold and beautiful part of Canada. Most Canadians don't live there because it is a hard place to get food and stay warm. Almost all Canadians live in the southern part of Canada, close to the USA. However, there are many things that are special about Canada's Arctic.

Northern Canada is divided into (に分け) 3 areas: The Northwest Territories, The Yukon, and Nunavut. Many native Canadians (先住民) live there. It is the coldest part of Canada.

In winter, around December 21-22, it is dark for more than 24 hours. It is the darkest time of the year. The sun does not come up into the sky. It is called the Polar Night. In summer, around June 21, the sun is in the sky for 24 hours. It is called the Midnight Sun, and some people don't sleep well at this time of the year.

There are 5 oceans in the world, and 3 of them touch Canada. The Arctic Ocean is the coldest and the smallest ocean in the world.

Some people say the Arctic is the most beautiful place in Canada. But it is not always easy to live there. The ground is almost always frozen. People there can't grow food in the ground.

The Inuit are the native people who live near the Arctic. In summer, many Inuit live in tents, and in winter, they live in houses made from soil (土壌). When the Inuit hunt (狩る), they build ice homes called igloos.

The Arctic Ocean has a lot of ice that covers the water. Polar bears, seals, and arctic foxes live on the ice. If the ice melts, these animals will lose their home.

The Arctic is the only place in the world to see polar bears and it is a beautiful place to watch the Aurora Borealis. Every year, thousands of Japanese tourists visit cities like Yellowknife to see the spectacular Aurora Borealis. They can experience life in one of the coldest and most amazing parts of the world.

1 Understanding the Story

Read the sentences below and decide if they are true (真) or false (偽)

(1)   The Arctic Ocean is in the south part of Canada.   _____

(2)   The Polar Night is a dark time in the Arctic.   _____

(3)   Igloos are made out of soil.   _____

(4)   Quebec is not the biggest province in Canada.   _____

(5)   The Inuit make igloos when they go hunting.   _____

2 Let's Practice...Adjectives

Adjectives are words that describe people, places, and things.

From the list below, which adjectives use er/est and which use more/most?

Generous: _____*more/most*_____   Talented: _____

Short: _____   Boring: _____

Fast: _____   Interesting: _____

Expensive: _____   Kind: _____

Quiet: _____   Funny: _____

Difficult: _____   Cold: _____

Loud: _____   Fun: _____

Cheap: _____   Intelligent: _____

Exercise 1: Describing

Pick one person in the room you are in. After you finish, read out your description. The other people in the room have to guess who the person is.

1. This person is _____

2. This person has _____

3. This person never _____

4. This person likes _____

Exercise 2: Comparing
Look at these pictures, and compare the people in the pictures.
FOR EXAMPLE: The man on the left is SHORTER THAN the man on the right.

1 Answer: _____

2 Answer: _____

3 Answer: _____

4 Answer: _____

3 Writing Practice: Making Questions

All of the sentences below are NOT correct. Try to make a perfect question by using all of the words in the sentence.

ヒント

Tallest Japan what building the is in?
Answer: What is the tallest building in Japan?

1. Coldest in what Japan city the is?

   _____

2. Largest country what is world the in the?

   _____

3. TV show is most what interesting in Japan the?

   _____

4. Who you taller is than you this class in?

   _____

5. [For living] Most what expensive in city the world the is?

   _____

Unit 4
Canada's Only Desert

Warm-up Questions

1. Can you describe a desert (weather, land, animals...)?

2. Have you ever been to a desert?

3. What is your favourite dessert?

4. If you went to a desert, what would you bring?

5. Some big cities, like Las Vegas, are in deserts. Would you like to live there?

Write the correct word for the pictures below.

Dry, temperature, rare, border, cactus, owl, rides, sound like a rattlesnake, farmers

1. _____ 2. _____ 3. _____ 4. _____ 5. _____

The Osoyoos Desert

A desert is not something we eat after dinner. It is a dry place. There is not a lot of rain in a desert. There is only one desert in Canada, and it is called The Osoyoos Desert. The Osoyoos Desert is in British Columbia near the U.S. border.

In summer, the temperature is around 38C, and in winter, it can be close to 1C. All year long, the Osoyoos desert is dry, but it rains about 93 days a year. In Vancouver, it rains about 165 days a year.

The Osoyoos Desert is one of the hottest places in Canada, but many plants grow there. In this desert, there are many rare plants like different kinds of cactus. Some of the plants and flowers that grow in this desert are in no other place (他の場所で) in the world. The Mariposa lily is one of these rare desert plants, and so is the woodland star.

There are around 100 rare plants and 300 animals that only live in the Osoyoos Desert. The painted turtle and the burrowing owl are two famous animals that live in this desert.

The burrowing owl lives under the ground. It sleeps in other animals' homes. These owls are very smart, too. A burrowing owl can sound like a rattlesnake to scare away (追い払う) any danger.

In the city of Osoyoos, there are around 6 700 people. It is a small city. One of the people who lives there is John Middleton. He moved to the city many years ago. He wanted to live a quiet life. He lives in a house on a mountain above the desert. Sometimes, he rides his horse around the town.

There are many things for people to do in Osoyoos. People can go horseback riding, play golf, or relax. People can visit Lake Osoyoos, the warmest lake in Canada. These days, many businesses grow grapes and make wine in Osoyoos. But there is one problem. Rattlesnakes love to eat grapes, and many farmers have to be careful when they pick their grapes.

1   Understanding the Story

Use the words below to complete the story.

plants, grapes, desert, owl, horses, under, close to, in

The Osoyoos _____ is in British Columbia. It is _____ the US

border. _____ summer, it is usually the hottest place in Canada. In this desert,

there are many special animals and _____. One animal is called the burrowing

_____. It lives _____ the ground and can make a rattlesnake sound.

Some people in the city of Osoyoos ride their _____ around the city, and some

people grow _____. They are delicious, and we can make wine with them.

2   Let's Practice...Prepositions of Place

We use prepositions of place to tell us where something is, or where it is going:

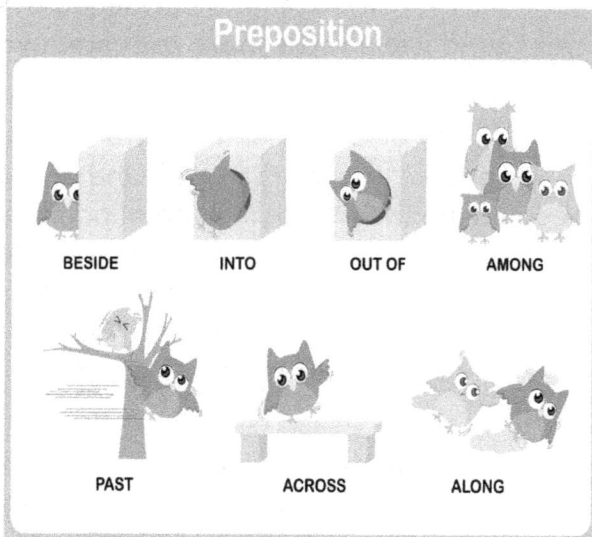

Preposition

BESIDE   INTO   OUT OF   AMONG

PAST   ACROSS   ALONG

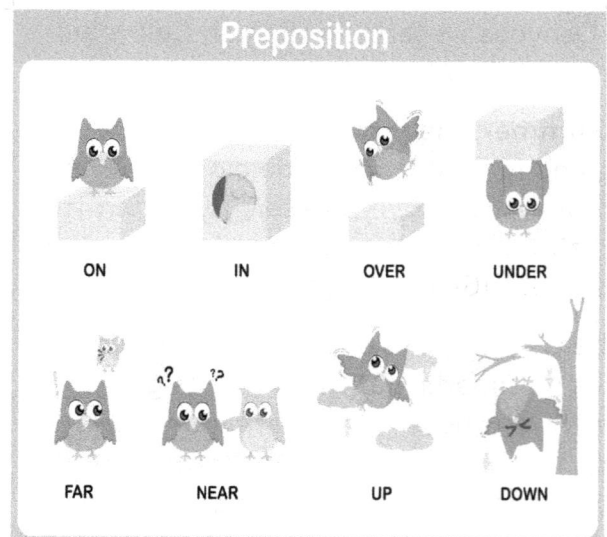

Preposition

ON   IN   OVER   UNDER

FAR   NEAR   UP   DOWN

ヒント
- The boy ran PAST the tree.
- Mexico is IN North America.
- I want to walk ALONG the Nile River.
- There is a hospital BESIDE my home.
- The girl jumped INTO the swimming pool.

3 Let's Practice...More Prepositions of Place

Finish the sentences below using the correct preposition. Not all of the answers are on page 24, so try to answer some of the questions with other prepositions, for example, *between* or *in front of*.

1. The clock is _____ the wall.

2. The fork is _____ the girl's hand.

3. The cat is standing _____.

4. The table is _____ the chairs.

5. The cat door is _____ the clock.

6. The window is _____ the bear.

7. The clouds are _____ the sky.

8. The trees are _____ the window.

9. The girl is sitting _____ from the bear.

10. The curtains are _____ the window.

4 Sentence Order

Read the sentences below, and put the story in the right order. Write a number next to the sentence in the order it happens. There are 10 sentences, and the first is already done.

_____ There was a lot of snow on the ground, but Yuki didn't like snow.

_____ She had lots of fun on her trip.

_____ First, Yuki went to a hotel. Next, she looked around the city.

_____ The man answered, "You should go to the Osoyoos Desert by bus."

_____ Osoyoos City was very beautiful, with nice buildings and warm weather.

_____ Yuki went to an airport, and got on a plane.

_____ Yuki was cold, so she asked a man, "Where is a warm place in Canada?"

_____ So, Yuki got on a bus, and went to the desert.

___1___ One day, Yuki was bored, so she took a trip to Canada.

_____ When she arrived in Canada, she was surprised.

Unit 5

Canada's van Gogh

Warm-up Questions

1. How many (幾つ) paintings do you have in your home?

2. Can you draw (描く) well?

3. If you could buy any painting, which one would you buy?

4. Do you collect (収集する) anything?

5. How often (どのくらいの頻度で) do you go to a museum?

VOCABULARY

Match the words in the vocabulary with the Japanese words below.

Not as famous as, mysteriously, famous, paint, nature, forests, sick, quit his job, canoe

1. 森 ： _____

2. ペイントする ： _____

3. カヌー ： _____

4. 仕事を辞め ： _____

5. 有名な ： _____

6. 病人 ： _____

7. 自然 ： _____

Tom Thompson

Sadly, many great artists die young. Even though Tom Thompson is not as famous as painters like Van Gogh or Vermeer, he is one of Canada's most important artists. Thompson died young, and he also died mysteriously.

Tom Thompson is one of the most famous Canadian artists in the world. Some people call him Canada's Van Gogh, and his paintings are in a lot of museums. He painted the beautiful nature in Canada. For many years, he painted in a park in Ontario called Algonquin Park. In 1917, he died mysteriously. He was only 39 years old. He had no wife and no children.

When he was young, he liked to walk in forests, up mountains, and along beaches. He helped his father's friend pick (選り抜く) special plants in Canada's forests. He learned plenty of things about nature at this time.

Even though (たとえ) he liked to walk in forests, he was a sick child, and he did not go to high school. When he was young, he started to paint, and when he was around 20 years old, he moved to Seattle (シアトルに移動). He worked in an art company, and he was happy. Most of his friends in Seattle were artists, too. But something happened to him that changed his life (自分の人生を変えた).

Thompson was dating a young lady, and he asked her to marry him. She said no. Thompson was so sad that he quit his job, and went back to Canada. On the train to Toronto from Seattle, he decided to become an artist.

When he was 37 years old, he lived in Algonquin Park from spring (春) to fall (秋). All of his paintings were about nature at this time.

One day in 1917, Tom Thompson went into a canoe to go fishing. It was a beautiful summer day. He was alone (独り) in his canoe. A few hours after he left, somebody found (発見) his canoe. Nobody was in it. One week later, somebody found his body in the lake. His death is still a mystery (謎).

In his life, Thompson painted around 50 canvases and 300 sketches.

1   Understanding the Story

Answer the following questions.

1.   What do some people call Tom Thompson?

_____

2.   How many paintings did he paint?

_____

3.   Where did he draw his paintings?

_____

4.   What did he like to paint?

_____

5.   Why did he move back to Canada?

_____

2   Looking at Grammar: Quantifiers

We use quantifiers when we talk about amounts (量). Some of these words can be used with counting nouns, non-counting nouns, or both.

| ヒント | • For big groups: Most people, All elephants |
| | • For specific (特定) groups: Most of the people (in this class), all of the elephants (in this zoo) |

Quantity	Meaning	Counting Nouns	N/C Nouns
No*	0%	Yes	Yes
One	1	Yes	No
A few	2 or 3	Yes	No
Several	more than 2, but not many	Yes	No
Some	a small number	Yes	Yes
Half*	50% of something	Yes	Yes
Many	a big number	Yes	No
Much	a big amount	No	Yes
A lot of	a large number or amount	Yes	Yes
A great deal of	a large amount	No	Yes
Plenty of	a large number or amount	Yes	Yes
Most	a large number	Yes	Yes
All	100%	Yes	Yes

3 Let's Practice...'How Many' Questions

Exercise 1 - Answer the sentences below using the words on page 28.

1. How many people in this class are Japanese? _____

2. How many people in the world can fly? _____

3. How many glasses of water do you drink every day? _____

4. How many people in your family drive a car? _____

5. How many of your friends live in a foreign country? _____

Exercise 2 - Finish the sentences using the words below.

A few, a little, many, much, a lot of, plenty of, hardly any, enough

1. Do you eat _____ rice?

2. I have 1000 pens, so I have _____ pens. I don't need more.

3. How _____ people live in this city?

4. How _____ money do you have in your wallet?

5. Only _____ people came to my party, so I was sad.

6. I have _____ time, so I must hurry.

7. I have _____ free time, so I can relax everyday.

8. Yasuko has 100 apples, but Yumi has _____ apples (just 2).

9. He has as _____ friends as me (same number of friends).

10. I like ice cream as _____ as you (same).

4 Writing : Describing My City

Describe your city using the words studied in this unit. There can be many different answers.

I live in _____. In my city, there are a lot of _____ and many

_____. Near my house, there are plenty of _____, so I am happy. I

think there are enough _____, so my city doesn't need more. Also, I feel there are

too many _____. I don't like them because _____.

My city has hardly any _____, so I wish there were more of them.

Unit 6

Money

Warm-up Questions

1. How much money do you have in your wallet right now?

2. What do you spend money on (金を使う)?

3. What do you think is expensive in Japan?

4. Are you good at saving money? If yes, how do you save money?

5. If you had no money, what would you do?

VOCABULARY

Finish the story with the words from the vocabulary list below.

Baseball, antique, especially, valuable, bills, collect, hobby, quit, rare, check, worth

I like to _____ things. It is not my job. It is just my _____. One day, I was walking in a park. _____ was in the park, so it was quiet. Under a tree, I saw a box. The box was new, it wasn't an _____, so I picked it up and opened it. Inside, there were no coins but many _____. I was shocked. I took the money to a police station. The policeman said the box was very _____. In 1 week, I will find out if the box is mine. Maybe in the future, I can _____ my job.

Canada's Most Expensive Coin

All over the world, people like to collect things. Some people collect baseball cards, comic books, stamps or even antique cars. But one of the most popular things to collect is money, especially coins.

Canada has 6 kinds of coins and 5 kinds of bills. The penny (or cent) is the lowest coin (.01), and the toonie is the highest ($2).

Queen Elizabeth is on all Canadian coins. When the king or queen of England changes, the Bank of Canada changes the picture on the coins. In the past, Queen Elizabeth looked very young on Canadian coins.

People who collect coins are called coin collectors. That is their hobby. The most valuable Canadian coin was made in 1936. It is a penny. It was worth 1 cent, and it is similar to a 1 yen coin (円硬貨). But in the world, there are only 3 of these coins, so it is very special.

The 1936 penny has an interesting story.

When Queen Elizabeth's grandfather died in 1936, the Bank of Canada started to make new coins. The next king was Edward, but he had a problem. He loved an American woman, but she had divorced two times. People in England worried. Would the next Queen of England be a woman divorced two times, and an American?

So after 300 days, Edward stopped being King of England. He quit the job. Edward's younger brother became king in 1936.

The Bank of Canada now had a problem. Nobody had a good photo of the new king. So for a very short time, the Bank of Canada made pennies with the dead king's picture on them. There was a dot under 1936.

In 1937, the new king's photo was put on Canadian coins. The 1936 dot pennies with the dead king's photo are very rare. In 2013, a Canadian coin collector paid $250 000 dollars to buy one. In Japanese yen, the man paid about ¥23 357 261.

If you go to Canada, and find an old penny, you should check the date. Maybe it will be worth more than 1 cent.

1 Understanding the Story

Answer the following questions.

1.   How many coins does Canada use?

_____

2.   What is the .01 Canadian coin called?

_____

3.   Why did King Edward stop being king?

_____

4.   Who can we see on Canadian coins?

_____

5.   Why was the 1936 Canadian penny so expensive?

_____

2 Let's Practice...Talking about the Past

First, try to describe what is happening in each picture.
Next, try to answer the questions for each photo.

Picture 1 Description

_____

_____

_____

1.   What made them so angry?

_____

2.   How often do you think they fight?

_____

Picture 2 Description

_____

_____

_____

1.   What did they do yesterday?

- -

2.   How might he pay for the ring?

- -

Picture 3 Description

_____

_____

_____

1.   Where did they go yesterday?

- -

2.   How long did it take to get there?

- -

Picture 4 Description

_____

_____

_____

1.   What did they eat for breakfast?

- -

2.   How do you like your eggs?

- -

3 **Writing : HOW Questions**

First, make a perfect question with the scrambled words. Then, answer each of the questions.

ヒント

Old are how you? = How old are you?

Answer: I am 26 years old.

1. Many how in live hometown your people?

Question: _____?

Answer: _____.

2. Are tall you how?

Question: _____?

Answer: _____.

3. Water everyday how drink much you do?

Question: _____?

Answer: _____.

4. Your is how bed big?

Question: _____?

Answer: _____.

5. Like you steak do? About how hamburgers?

Question: _____?

Answer: _____.

6. Cost your does how watch much?

Question: _____?

Answer: _____.

7. You today did come how here?

Question: _____?

Answer: _____.

8. How here is home far your from?

Question: _____?

Answer: _____.

4   Discussion

Ask the 8 questions on page 34 to a partner. Write down his or her answers in the space below. Then ask your partner one bonus question. The question should be about your partner's answer to the first question. Or it can be similar to the question you asked.

ヒント   Question 1: *How many people live in your hometown?*
Question 2: *How many people are there in your family?*

1. _____
_____

2. _____
_____

3. _____
_____

4. _____
_____

5. _____
_____

6. _____
_____

7. _____
_____

8. _____
_____

Unit 7

Religion: Buddhism

Warm-up Questions

1. What do you think is difficult about a monk's job?

2. Have you ever been to India? If no, would you like to go?

3. What do you think makes people happy?

4. Are you greedy (貪欲な) about anything (money, food...)?

5. What do you sometimes worry about?

VOCABULARY

Use the correct word to finish the sentences.

Disappear, traditions, greedy, suffer, temple, monk, outside, servant, homeless, meditate

1. It's nice _____. I want to go fishing.

2. I don't like to clean my home. I wish I had a _____.

3. _____ people are cold in winter.

4. When people _____, they look relaxed.

5. _____ people always want more things.

The Life of Buddha

In the late 1800s, Japanese Buddhists in Canada were worried. They thought that Japanese culture and traditions were disappearing. So, they did 2 things.

First, they built a temple. Second, they invited a monk from Japan to work at the temple. On December 12, 1905, a Jodo Shinshu temple was built, and it was the first Buddhist temple in Canada.

Buddhism began around 500BC by a prince in India. His name was Siddhartha. When he was born, his mother died 2 days after. Siddhartha's father was very sad.

Siddhartha's life was very good. In his childhood, he was very kind to animals. He was the best student in his class, and he was very good at games.

His life was good and very easy. But he wanted to help other people.

He was happy, but he knew that many people and animals suffer (苦しむ) in life. He asked his father about poor people, but his father told him to think about other things.

The king worried about Siddhartha. He did not want his son to think too deeply (深く考える) about life. The king also worried about his son's future. He didn't want his son to become a monk.

After he married, Siddhartha learned about the world outside his castle. His servant Channa helped him. Channa taught Siddhartha about getting old, getting sick, and death. Siddhartha didn't want people to suffer.

One day, he left his home and family. He became a homeless monk. He wanted to understand (理解したかった) life and suffering.

In one village, he spoke to a group of people, "If you want to be happy, you can't hurt any creatures (生き物). People who kill will be killed (殺される)." Siddhartha studied many things, sometimes didn't eat, and always wanted to learn how to stop suffering.

One day, while he was meditating (座禅・瞑想), he learned that suffering starts when people are greedy.

Finally, he learned the answer. He found nirvana (涅槃). When he was 35 years old, he became Buddha.

1   Understanding the Story

Answer the following questions.

1.   To Buddhists, why do people suffer?

   _____

2.   What kind of life did Siddhartha have?

   _____

3.   When was the first Buddhist temple in Canada built?

   _____

4.   How old was Siddhartha when he became Buddha?

   _____

2   Listening Practice: Routines

Listen and answer the questions to the upside-down story.

Sunday is my holiday. On Sunday, I wake up early in the morning, and take a walk with my dog. If the weather is nice, we go for a long walk. Sometimes, we walk to the Toyohira River, and sometimes we walk around Nakajima Park. After that, I eat a delicious breakfast, and take a shower. In the afternoon, I like to study or read a book. Sometimes, I play golf with my friends. In the evening, I eat dinner with my whole family. Every Sunday night, I talk with my mom, and then watch some TV. Finally, I get ready for bed, and sleep early.

Questions

1.   Where do I go on Sunday morning?
2.   What kind of breakfast do I eat?
3.   When do I take a shower?
4.   What do I do in the afternoon?
5.   Who do I eat dinner with?
6.   Do I watch TV before I talk with my mom?

3   Looking at Grammar: *Tell/Say/Ask/Speak*

These 4 verbs have similar meanings, but are used in different ways;

ヒント   TELL – we usually say WHO is told.
   EXAMPLE: She told <u>me</u> to clean the room.

   SAY – we don't usually say who is told, but if you do use a person, use TO.
   EXAMPLE: He said something <u>to</u> his friend.

   ASK – use ASK for questions. Use IF with YES/NO questions.
   EXAMPLE: She <u>asked me if</u> I liked pizza (The girl asked me, "Do you like pizza?")

   SPEAK – use SPEAK for languages, how people talk, or speaking to a person.
   EXAMPLE: He speaks quietly (OR) She speaks three languages.

Finish the sentences using SAY, ASK, SPEAK or TELL.

1. He _____ me that he was tired.

2. He _____ goodbye to me.

3. Rex _____ to his friend yesterday.

4. She _____ in a quiet voice.

5. She _____ me for my phone number.

6. I _____ him if he wanted to go skiing.

7. I worried about her, so I _____ her to stop playing with the knife.

8. Yumi _____ the teacher for more homework. The other students were angry at her.

9. Yasuko can _____ 3 languages.

10. What did you _____? I didn't hear you.

4   Writing : Translation Practice

中央寺 の僧侶達は、毎朝早く起床します。お寺は、僧侶たちの訓練の場所です。中央寺僧堂では、15人の僧侶達が生活しています。その大きな建物内には、たくさんの部屋と仏像があり、多くの花が飾られています。お寺の長である方丈様は、非常に賢明な方です。方丈様は、優れた僧侶になる方法を説法しています。僧侶として生きる事は重要な仕事である。私は彼らを尊敬しているし、その髪型が大好きです。

Read the story above and change it into English. It is about a Buddhist temple called Chuo Ji.

_____

_____

_____

_____

_____

_____

_____

_____

_____

Unit 8
Halifax Explosion, 1917

Warm-up Questions

1. Have you had a fire in your home?

2. Have you ever been in danger?

3. What do you think about (あなたはどう思いますか) traveling on boats?

4. Can you swim well?

5. How many accidents (i.e. car, bicycle) have you had in your life?

VOCABULARY

Use the correct word to finish the sentences.

Caught fire, TNT, put out the fire, port, hit, each other, explosion, bombs, shore, burn

1. Anne and Diana play games with _____.

2. You can see many boats at a _____.

3. I dropped the TNT, but happily, there was no _____.

4. Sometimes a _____ doesn't have sand, but a beach does.

5. Boxers try to _____ each other hard.

The Great Halifax Explosion

On a beautiful, sunny day in 1917, two boats crashed into each other. One of the boats caught fire. There was a problem. The boat was carrying a lot of TNT, and the sailors couldn't put out the fire. The ship exploded, hurting and killing thousands of people in Halifax, Canada.

Halifax is a port city on the east coast of Canada. A port is a place where boats go, like Hakodate and Yokohama. It can be a dangerous place because some of the boats are very big. Almost 100 years ago, in Halifax, two boats hit each other. There was a very big explosion, and many people died. It is still the biggest accident in Canadian history.

Halifax is a city in Nova Scotia. During World War 1, Halifax was an important harbour (港) and port town. Food, guns, bombs and soldiers were brought to Halifax for the war. Then they went to Europe by ship. The SS Mont Blanc was one of these ships. The Mont Blanc was from France, and it was bringing guns and bombs to Europe.

On December 6th, 1917, the SS Mont Blanc sailed into Halifax Harbour. It was a beautiful, sunny day, but the French ship hit another ship. The SS Mont Blanc started to burn. There was a fire on the ship.

People close to the harbour and people in the city went to watch the burning ship. Many people wanted to see what was happening. They didn't know there was any danger.

The Mont Blanc moved closer to the shore. The French sailors were yelling at the people. They told them to run away. But the sailors spoke French. The people in Halifax didn't understand what they were saying.

When the ship was very close to (近くに) the shore, it exploded. On the ship, there were 2 989 tons of TNT. The ship was destroyed (破壊された). Many buildings around Halifax Port were also destroyed, and many buildings in the city caught fire. Two thousand people died in the explosion or in the fires, and about 9000 people were injured (負傷した).

41

1   Understanding the Story

Answer the following questions.

1.   What is a port?

      _____

2.   Why did the French ship sail to Halifax?

      _____

3.   Why did people in Halifax go to the port?

      _____

4.   Why didn't the people watching the boat run away?

      _____

5.   How much TNT was on The Mont Blanc?

      _____

2   Let's Practice...There is / It is

We use There is when we talk about something being or existing (既存の) in a place.

ヒント	• There is a bank close to here. • There are 14 chairs in this room. • There are a lamp, 2 tables and a fan in this room.

We use It is when we talk about things like the weather, to identify (識別する) something, to talk about time, and to talk about distance (距離).

ヒント	• It is cold today. (NOT There is cold today) • What is it? It is a bird. • What time is it? It is 5 o'clock. • How far is it to the airport? It's about 30 minutes to the airport (OR It takes about 30 minutes to the airport)

Exercise 1

Finish the sentences or circle the answer the questions below using IS / ARE.

1. <u>There is / There are / It is</u> many chairs in this room.

2. <u>There is / It is</u> some tea in my cup.

3. <u>There / It</u> is an old cup.

4. There <u>are / is</u> many books on the table.

5. There <u>are / is</u> a clock, tables, and chairs in this room.

6. <u>It / There</u> is very late. Maybe we should go home.

7. <u>There is / It is</u> a rose on the table. I think <u>there is / it is</u> yours.

8. Do you like that painting? <u>There is / It is</u> by Vermeer.

9. This hotel is cheap, but <u>there is / it is</u> a nice swimming pool inside.

10. What day is it? _____

11. How far is it from your home to this building? _____

12. How is the weather today? _____

Exercise 2

All of these sentences are not correct (正しくない). Read and fix the sentences.

1. There is many book at the bag.

   _____

2. It is a lots of money at the brown, big bag.

   _____

3. It is letter on table for me mom.

   _____

4. He spoke me that there is 2pm o'clock.

   _____

5. There is a sun day today, but let us go to outside.

   _____

Unit 9

The Titanic

Warm-up Questions

1. When was the last time you took a boat?

2. Have you ever had a bad vacation?

3. What is dangerous about traveling by boat?

4. What is the nicest hotel you have stayed in?

5. What is your favourite kind of transportation (交通)?

VOCABULARY

Use the correct word to finish the sentences.

Embarrassed, sailor, skilled at, luxurious, sank, survive, tried to, lifeboat, coward, passenger

1. Yesterday, I _____ climb a mountain, but it was too hard.

2. He is afraid of everything, even butterflies. I think he is a _____.

3. The boat _____ in the river, but nobody was hurt.

4. She is a _____, and she is _____ sailing boats.

5. I would like to buy a _____ watch, but I have no money.

The Titanic

The Titanic was the most famous, most expensive, and most beautiful ship ever made. On its first trip, it sailed to New York.

When the Titanic was built in 1912, nobody thought it could sink. One of the sailors on the Titanic told passengers, "God himself couldn't sink this ship." The captain of the Titanic was very skilled at sailing, and was never in a sailing accident his whole life. But it did sink, and it happened very close to Canada.

There were many famous and rich people from England on the ship, and there was also one Japanese man.

On April 14th, 1912, the Titanic hit an iceberg at 11:40 pm close to Newfoundland and Nova Scotia. At 2:20 am, the ship began to sink. Many people on the ship didn't survive.

There were around 2,200 passengers on the ship. About 700 people were in third class. They had to sleep at the bottom of the ship. These tickets weren't expensive. The people in 1st class were rich. At that time, these tickets cost around $25,000 USD.

The Titanic had the nicest swimming pool, the most delicious food, and the best rooms on any ship in the world. But this was for passengers in 1st class. Second and third class passengers did not have the same luxuries. And this is where the Japanese passenger stayed, in a 2nd class cabin.

Masabumi Hosono didn't die in the accident, but his life changed after it. At that time, he worked for the Japanese government, and was going back to Japan. When the Titanic hit the iceberg, Hosono was sleeping. He woke up about 30 minutes after the ship hit the iceberg. He tried to get on a lifeboat three times, but he couldn't get a seat.

Finally, he got lucky. He got on one of the last lifeboats. He was safe. He was one of the luckiest people on the ship.

But in Japan, newspapers called him a coward. Soon, he lost his job. In schoolbooks, stories about Hosono said he embarrassed Japan. Some people even said he should commit hara-kiri.

Until he died in 1939, he never talked about what happened on the Titanic. It was the worst thing to happen to him in his life.

1   Understanding the Story

Answer the questions below from the story, 'The Titanic'.

1.   What does it mean, "God himself couldn't sink this ship"?
a) The Titanic was big   b) The Titanic was strong   c) The Titanic was expensive

2.   Where was the Titanic going?
a) New York   b) Newfoundland   c) Nova Scotia

3.   If somebody doesn't survive, it means the person _____.
a) dead   b) died   c) death

4.   Hosono tried to get onto a lifeboat _____ times.
a) 3   b) 4   c) 5

5.   For Hosono, it was the _____ thing to happen to him in his life.
a) hardest   b) longest   c) worst

2   Looking at Grammar: Helping Verbs

In the story, we read that Hosono didn't die, and that the 3rd class tickets weren't expensive.
These are negative sentences, and they use Helping Verbs.

ヒント   Helping Verbs are always followed by a regular verb.

Exercise 1:   Circle the right answer that describes the picture.

Picture 1   A) You can stop!
                 B) You should stop!
                 C) You must stop!

Picture 2   Tomorrow, it
                 A) won't rain
                 B) isn't rain
                 C) is not going to rain

Picture 3   A) He had better not study.
             B) He didn't study.
             C) He can't study.

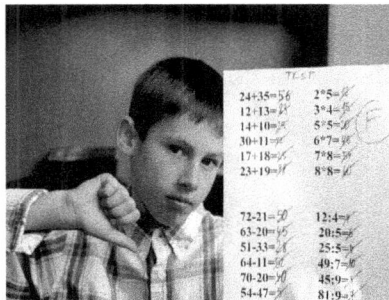

Exercise 2: Finish the following sentences using these negative helping verbs.

   Aren't, isn't, can't, couldn't, didn't, don't, had better not, mustn't, shouldn't, won't

1. You _____ oversleep, or else your boss will be very angry.

2. Shinzo _____ fly.

3. Yoko _____ do her homework, so the teacher was upset.

4. I am sorry I _____ go to your wedding. I was very sick.

5. I think it _____ rain tomorrow, so let's go to the park.

6. Yumiko and Mayumi _____ dumb, they are very smart.

7. Hideyuki and Masao _____ drink *sake* for breakfast.

8. My teacher is short. He _____ tall.

9. Sumie and Kiyoe _____ enjoy working on Saturday.

10. If you _____ finish your work, we _____ go to Hawaii tomorrow.

3   Writing : Translation Practice

Try to translate this short story into English.

昨日、私は私の車を運転ていました。私は良いドライバーですが、事故に遭いました。私の車がトラックに衝突したのです。私は 首を怪我しました。医者に見せる必要があったので、病院に行きました。彼は怪我ではないとおっしゃりました。私の車は故障がひどく、タクシーで家に帰りました。

_____

_____

_____

_____

_____

_____

Unit 10

Japanese People in Canada

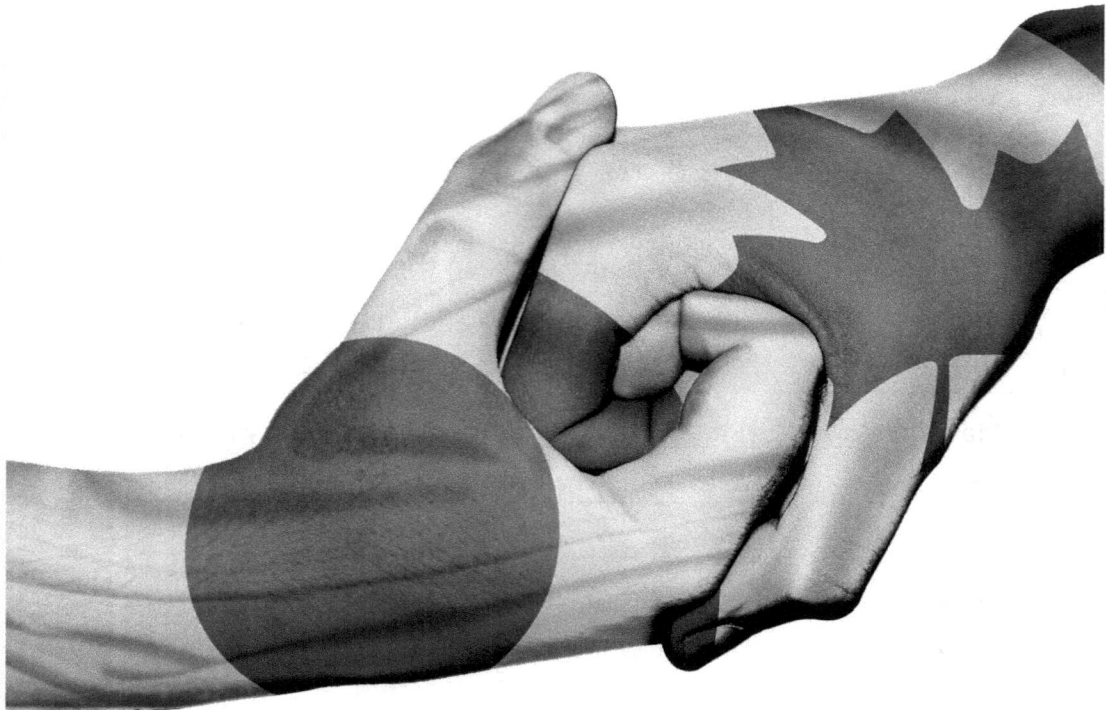

Warm-up Questions

1. Do you have any friends living in a foreign country?

2. Which country wouldn't you like to live in?

3. Where is the nicest place you have lived?

4. How many times have you moved in your life?

5. If you moved to Canada, where would you like to live?

Match the words in the vocabulary with the Japanese words below.

Immigrate, several, made up his mind, move to, returned, weak, burned down,

lonely, desire, named after

1. 寂しい:_____

2. いくつかの:_____

3. 決定する:_____

4. 移住:_____

5. 弱い : _____

6. 戻ってくる : _____

7. 欲望 : _____

Manzo Nagano

Moving to a new country is not easy. Learning a new language, having no friends, and living in a strange culture can make a person's life difficult. And for one Japanese man, moving to Canada was even more difficult. He was the first Japanese person to immigrate to Canada, and his name was Manzo Nagano.

There are several famous Japanese Canadians from Vancouver. For example, the TV host/environmentalist David Suzuki, and the great hockey player Paul Kariya. However, the first Japanese person to live in Vancouver didn't play hockey or help the environment. His name was Manzo Nagano.

When Manzo was 22 years old, he made up his mind to move to Canada. He sailed on a British ship from Yokohama to British Columbia. This was in 1877, and he was the first Japanese person to move to Canada.

In Canada, some people made fun of Manzo because he couldn't speak English. This didn't stop him from working. He was a fisherman at first, and then, he started an exporting business. He sent salmon back to Japan, and he made a lot of money.

In 1922, Manzo and his family had some bad luck. First, Manzo got sick, and it made him very weak. Next, his house and business burned down in a fire. His house and hotel were made of wood. He lost everything.

The next year, he returned to Japan. He died at the age of 68, but many of his family members still live in Canada.

Manzo Nagano left Japan with little money, no friends, and he could not speak English. In Canada, his life was hard and lonely. But his hard work and desire to succeed helped him make a good life in Canada. Manzo left Canada, but his name will always be remember.

In 1977, one hundred years after Manzo went to Canada, the Canadian government named a mountain after Manzo. It is in British Columbia's Coast Mountains, and its name is Mount Manzo Nagano.

1 Understanding the Story

Answer the questions below from the story, 'Manzo Nagano'.

1. Why did Manzo Nagano move to Canada?

   _____

2. Why did people make fun of him in Canada?

   _____

3. What happened to Manzo's house?

   _____

4. Where do many Japanese people live in Canada?

   _____

5. What kind of exporting business did Manzo have?

   _____

2 Let's Practice...Using *Made*

In the story about Manzo Nagano, MADE is used in many different ways: make money, make happy, make a good life, make fun of, make up his mind. With a partner, practice using the verb MADE.

Bonus Questions

1. Do you think it is easy or difficult to make money? _____

2. What makes you happy? _____

3. Did anyone make fun of you when you were young? _____

4. Do you make up your mind fast? _____

5. Where are your shoes made? _____

Exercise 1: Use the words below to finish the sentences.

   tea, trouble, friends, money, a phone call, your bed, a plan, a mistake, happy, study

1. I think Masao is a rich man. He makes a lot of _____.

2. I'm thirsty. Can you make some _____?

3. Every morning, Megumi makes her _____, so her bedroom is neat.

4. He is a bad man. He is always making _____.

5. Please wait. I have to make a _____ to my friend. Brrring brrring…

6. Kumiko is very shy. She doesn't make _____ easily.

7. If you want to escape from jail, you should make a good _____.

8. Junko's singing is soooo great. It always makes me _____.

9. When Hideko was young, her mom made her _____ on Sunday.

10. I think Sochika and Miyuma are nice. Whoops, I made a _____ . Sorry.

Exercise 2: Finish the following sentences using these prepositions: in, of, from, by, with

1. Keiko's bag is made _____ Italy.

2. Her car is made _____ Honda.

3. Her toilet is made _____ gold.

4. Her cake is made _____ butter.

5. Her notebook is made _____ wood.

3   Writing: Making Questions

Read the sentences. Make a question that answers each of the sentences. There is more than one answer for every question.

1. I make my wife happy by giving her flowers.

   How do you _____?

2. I make my bed every morning.

   How often _____?

3. I made a plan to exercise more this year.

   _____?

4. I don't make a lot of money.

   _____?

5. It makes me angry when I can't find my car keys.

   _____?

Unit 11

Newfoundland

Warm-up Questions

1. Newfoundland's nickname is The Rock. Do you have a nickname?

2. What do you dislike about living on an island?

3. What do you like about living on an island?

4. If you lived on an island for 1 year, what 3 things would you bring (except food & water)

5. Do you speak with an accent (or dialect)?

VOCABULARY

Write the correct word for the pictures below.

Similar to, continent, cod, flipper, nickname, crickets, skunks, porcupines, moose, float

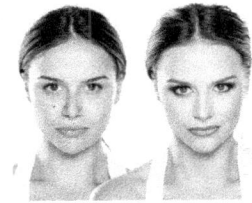

1. _____ 2. _____ 3. _____ 4. _____ 5. _____

The Rock

Newfoundland is a very special place in Canada. In 1949, Newfoundland joined Canada. It is the newest province (県) in the country. But it also has the oldest city in North America: St. John's. People in Newfoundland can see icebergs in summer. The people who live there speak English, but it is sometimes hard to understand them. Some people have an accent (強いアクセント).

Newfoundland is a little similar to Japan. Both countries are almost the same size (close to 400 000 km²). People in both places love fish, and both are in the east. Newfoundland is the easternmost (最東部) part of the North American continent.

Newfoundland has the oldest city in North America. It is called St. John's, and it is the capital city. Almost 40% of all people in Newfoundland live in this city. It was founded (設立) in 1497 by fishermen. In Canada, Newfoundland is famous for (で有名) fish.

People in Newfoundland eat some special food. One dish is cod tongue. It is almost always fried. Half of the tongue is like jelly,

and some people don't like to eat this part. Another famous dish from Newfoundland is seal flipper pie. Some people say it is very delicious.

Newfoundland has a nickname. It is called The Rock. However, forests cover over 33% of the island. In Newfoundland, there are no snakes, no crickets, no skunks, no deer and no porcupines. However, there are over 100 000 moose, so people need to be careful driving at night. Moose can weigh over 500kg, and cars that hit moose are badly damaged.

In summer, icebergs float past the island in May and June. Sadly, one of these icebergs hit the Titanic many years ago.

Many tourists in Newfoundland go to see the only Viking village in North America. It is a UNESCO World Heritage site.

One last thing that makes Newfoundland unique: it has its own time zone (時間帯), Newfoundland Time. It is 30 minutes different from Atlantic Time, and 11 hours and 30 minutes different from Japan Time.

1   Understanding the Story

Answer these questions about Newfoundland using full sentences.

1. When did Newfoundland join Canada??

_____

2. How is Newfoundland unique? (Give 1 answer)

_____

3. What is Newfoundland's nickname?

_____

4. How many porcupines live in Newfoundland?

_____

5. How much do moose weigh?

_____

2   Let's Practice...Stative Verbs

ヒント	Stative verbs don't usually use ING because we can't see the action happening. We <u>don't</u> say, "I am knowing you" because it is hard to see that action.

Here is a list of stative verbs that don't usually use ING:

Know, believe, remember, understand, like, love, dislike, fear, hate, belong, own, need, want, wish, hear, look like, agree, disagree, promise, surprise

Exercise 1: Use the verbs above to finish the sentences. Use the verbs only 1 time:

1. I _____ to buy a new fridge. My old fridge is broken.

2. I _____ your problem, but I can't help you.

3. She _____ a nice lady. She is always smiling.

4. (Hiding behind a door) "BOO!" "AH, you _____(d) me."

5. I _____ your phone number, so I will call you tomorrow.

6. This book _____ to me.

7. Every morning, I _____ a loud bell at 6am.

54

8. I _____ with you. She is a great singer.

9. Sokai _____ Takuro to help him cook dinner today.

10. I _____ I could take a holiday for 2 weeks.

Exercise 2: Using WANT. Write in your own ideas to finish the sentences.

1. He is hungry. He wants <u>TO EAT.</u> OR He wants <u>AN APPLE</u>.

2. She is thirsty. She wants _____.

3. It is snowing. I want _____.

4. They have no money. They want _____.

5. We are bored. We want _____.

6. I have a headache. I want _____.

7. My dog is barking. It wants _____.

8. My hair is long. I want _____.

9. His head is shiny. I want _____.

10. _____. I want to go shopping.

3 Discussion Topics

With a partner or in a group, discuss the following questions.

1. Which do you prefer, living in the city or countryside?

2. If tourists visited this city, where would you recommend (推奨する) them to go?

3. What kind of seafood do you like?

4. What do you dislike about your job?

5. What do you love to do on holidays?

Unit 12

Winnie the Pooh

Warm-up Questions

1. What is your favourite (望ましい) animal?

2. Did you have many toys/dolls when you were young?

3. How many pets have you had in your life (あなたの生活の中で)?

4. Do you have a favourite animation character?

5. What did you use to do when you were young?

Vocabulary

Match the words in the vocabulary to their meaning.

Woods, veterinarian, take care of, cub, called it, donated, adventures, at that time

1. To give : _____

2. To help : _____

3. Exciting actions _____

4. Many trees : _____

5. When that happened : _____

6. Give a name : _____

Pooh Bear

Winnie the Pooh is one of the most famous characters in the world. He was made from the imagination of an English writer, but the real Pooh grew up in the woods of Canada.

In 1914, Harry Colebourn was on a train going to Quebec. He was a veterinarian in the Canadian Army. He took care of horses, and loved animals. When the train stopped in White River, Ontario, he got off the train and walked around the small town.

He saw a hunter selling a baby bear. The hunter told him, "This bear has no mother. I'm selling this bear cub. Do you want to buy it?" Colebourn bought the bear for $20, and called it "Winnie" because Colebourn was from Winnipeg.

Winnie traveled to London with Colebourn and other soldiers. Winnie was the soldiers' mascot. When Colebourn had to go to France, he took Winnie to the London Zoo. He asked them to keep his bear until he came back to London.

At the zoo, Winnie became very popular. In 1920, Colebourn went back to Winnipeg, but he did not take the bear with him. He donated his bear to the zoo.

Winnie was the favourite animal to many young boys. One of the boys was Christopher Robins. Christopher liked the bear so much that he named his teddy bear Winnie. Christopher's father was a famous writer. His name was A. A. Milne.

Milne knew his son loved Winnie very much, so he decided to write a story for Christopher. In 1926, the 1st Winnie the Pooh story was published. It was a collection of short stories about Winnie's adventures in Hundred Acre Wood.

Millions of Winnie books were sold in many countries. Two of Winnie's fans were Walt Disney's daughters. They loved these stories. Walt Disney decided to make a movie about Winnie, and in 1977, Winnie the Pooh became a movie star. At that time, Winnie was the 2nd most popular Walt Disney character.

Winnie the bear became famous in London, England, but his real home was in the beautiful forests in Ontario, Canada.

1   Understanding the Story

Answer the following questions.

1.   How much did Colebourn pay for the bear cub?

_____

2.   Which province is Winnie the bear from?

_____

3.   In London, where did Winnie live?

_____

4.   When did Pooh become a movie star?

_____

5.   Which Disney character is the most popular?

_____

2   Let's Practice...Irregular Verbs

In the story about Winnie the Pooh, we can see many irregular verbs. These are verbs that DON'T take *ed* in the past tense. Here are the irregular verbs we studied in the story:

Be, become, buy, come, do, get, have, know, make, meet, see, sell, take, tell, write

Finish these sentences using the verbs above:

1.   Yesterday, I (meet) _____ my friend.

2.   Last week, I (buy) _____ some bread.

3.   Today, my teacher (come) _____ here at _____.

4.   Two years ago, I (take) _____ a trip to _____.

5.   The trip (be) _____ interesting because _____.

6.   In December, I (write) _____ postcards to _____.

7.   I (do) _____ my driver's license test in _____.

8.   My classmate (go) _____ to an *onsen* last _____.

9. Two years ago, I (sell) _____ my car for 500 000 ¥.

10. I (get) _____ home from work at 7pm, and then I (make) _____ dinner.

3 Writing : Translation

Here is a story about Yoko's trip to Canada. Try to translate it into English using the past tense verbs we studied in this unit.

昨年、陽子さんは、カナダのバンクーバーに旅行に行き、とても楽しい時間を過ごしました。陽子さんは、友達の伸三さんと旅行に行きました。陽子さん達は、きれいな景観を眺め、美味しい食事を楽しみ、沢山のお土産を買いました。マンゾー・ナガノ山へドライブに行った時、日本人観光客の人々に出会いました。陽子さんは、小熊を見かけたので、森の中に歩いて行きました。そこで、お母さん熊、グリズリー熊に遭遇しました。伸三さんは、履いていた靴をグリズリー熊に命中させ、二匹の熊は、逃げていきました。陽子さんは運が良く、伸三さんは、英雄的な活躍でした。

_____

_____

_____

_____

_____

_____

_____

_____

_____

_____

_____

Unit 13

Remembrance Day

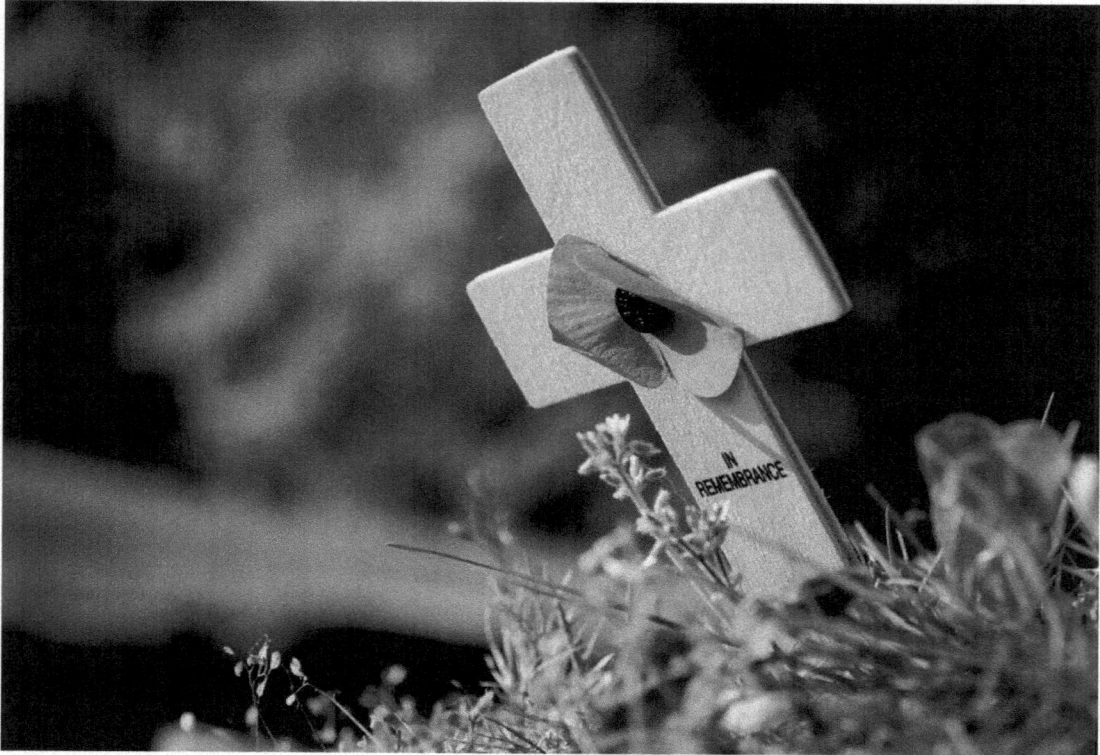

Warm-up Questions

1. Do you know anybody who is a soldier?

2. What do you think is difficult about being a soldier?

3. Have you ever fired a gun?

4. What do you usually do on holidays?

5. What don't you like to do on holidays?

VOCABULARY

Write the correct word for the pictures below.

Soldiers, dangerous, remember, fought for, ended, protect, grow, buy, wear, silent, conflicts

1. _____ 2. _____ 3. _____ 4. _____ 5. _____

Remembrance Day

Soldiers fight for (のために戦う) their countries. It is a hard and dangerous job, and sometimes soldiers die when countries go to war.

In 1914, WWI started in Europe. Canada was still ruled by the United Kingdom. So, Canadian soldiers fought in Europe with other British soldiers.

There were close to 7 million people living in Canada at that time. Over 200 000 soldiers died or were injured in this war.

In many countries, people remember the wars they fought. Canadians remember their soldiers on November 11th every year. On this day, World War I (WWI) ended. It is called Remembrance Day.

At 11 am on November 11th, ceremonies are held across Canada. They are serious ceremonies, and we can see and meet many soldiers at these events.

Ceremonies that are similar to Remembrance Day happen in other countries around the world on November 11th. World War I was a terrible war, and millions of people died because of it.

Almost 100 years ago, over 600 000 Canadians fought in WWI. In Belgium, a Canadian doctor wrote a poem (詩) about the war that became famous. He wrote the poem after his friend died. The poem's name is "In Flanders Field". Canadian students still learn this poem at school.

Poppies grow in Flanders Field in spring. So, before November 11, many Canadians buy and wear poppy pins on that day. At 11 am, on November 11, some Canadians stop speaking. They are silent, and try to remember the soldiers who died in that terrible war many years ago.

In 2014, there were 43 conflicts or wars happening in the world. Some of these fights are small, and some are large.

In the future, maybe there will be no more wars and there will be no more soldiers. If that happens, the world will be a more peaceful place to live. Do you think it is possible?

1   Understanding the Story

Answer the questions below from the reading, 'Remembrance Day'.

1.   When is Remembrance Day?

_____

2.   What flower do Canadians wear for Remembrance Day?

_____

3.   What do Canadians do on Remembrance Day at 11am?

_____

4.   Why is WWI important to Canadians?

_____

5.   How is the life of a soldier hard?

_____

2   Let's Practice...Expressions of Time

Time words such as *everyday*, *yesterday*, and *tomorrow* affect verb forms:

PAST EXPRESSIONS
- Yesterday (昨日), 2 days ago (二日前), last week (先週), in the past (昔), when I was young (私が若かったとき)

PRESENT EXPRESSIONS
- These days (近頃), everyday (毎日), right now (今), at this time (この時)

FUTURE EXPRESSIONS
- Tomorrow (明日), in 2 days (二日後), next month (来月), in the future (将来は), soon (間もなく)

Exercise 1: Answer the following questions in full sentences. Ask a partner the same questions.

1.   What are you doing right now?

_____

2.   What do you drink everyday?

_____

3.   Where did you go yesterday?

_____

4. What were you doing last night at 11pm?

_____

5. Tomorrow, who will you meet?

_____

6. What will you be doing tonight at 9pm?

_____

Exercise 2: Answer the following questions using the correct expression of time on pg. 62.

1. _____, Tokugawa was the Shogun of Japan.

2. Kaori is studying English _____.

3. _____, I will be an old man.

4. We will say goodbye _____.

5. _____, (Saturday) it rained.

6. _____, the weather is cool at night.

7. _____, Nagano has lots of snow.

8. _____, the winter Olympics were in Tokyo.

3   Sentence Order: What Happened First?

Read the sentences below about the history of Japan. Put them in the right order, with #1 the oldest and # 9 the newest.

_____ Emperor Meiji makes Japan a powerful and rich country.

__1__ Buddhism comes to Japan.

_____ John Lennon and Yoko Ono get married

_____ Shoguns rule Japan.

_____ The Summer Olympics are in Tokyo for the first time.

_____ The Great Kanto earthquake destroys Tokyo and Yokohama.

_____ Yukawa Hideki is the first Japanese to win the Nobel Prize in physics.

_____ Okinawa is returned to Japan by Americans

_____ General Perry forces Japan to trade with the US.

Unit 14

Wish You A
Merry Christmas

Warm-up Questions

1. How are you similar to Santa?

2. What kind of presents do you like to get?

3. What is the best gift you have ever received (受け取る)?

4. What do you usually do at Christmas?

5. How often do you go to a church (教会) or temple (寺) or shrine (神社) to pray?

VOCABULARY

Answer the questions below.

Celebrate, differences, fake, donate, turkey, churches, filled with, during, probably, open gifts

1. What is your fridge filled with? _____

2. How often do you eat turkey? _____

3. During a movie, what do you like to do? _____

4. What will you probably do tomorrow? _____

Christmas

There are many special holidays in Canada, but one of the most special is Christmas. For some people, it is a religious (宗教的な) day. For others, it is a time to give gifts, meet family members, and eat delicious food.

Christmas is celebrated on December 25th around the world. But there are some differences in how people celebrate (祝う) Christmas.

In Canada, many people like to buy pine trees, or use fake (偽) trees. People put a l of their presents under the tree, and wait until (まで) Christmas day to open the gifts. Canadians also like to donate money, food, and gifts at this time of the year.

On Christmas Eve, the streets are quiet. Almost no stores or restaurants are open. But churches are very busy on Christmas Eve. Usually, the churches are filled with people. People go to church to pray.

Young children believe in (信じる) Santa Claus. They hope to get many presents on Christmas Day. During the year (年無い), mothers tell their children, "If you want to get presents, you must be good, or else (ある

いは) Santa will give you no presents!"

So, many children try to be very good, especially (特に) close to Christmas. Terrible children, their mothers tell them, don't get presents at Christmas time.

Children write letters to Santa asking for presents. Canadians believe Santa lives in the Arctic, close to the North Pole (北極).

Christmas is also a time when families meet. In many families, mothers cook delicious food like turkey and ham, potatoes and carrots, and everybody eats a lot of food. Families also listen to Christmas songs.

'We Wish You a Merry Christmas' is an old English Christmas carol (キャロル). It was probably written more than 400 years ago. On Christmas Eve, groups of people walked around their neighbourhood (近所) and sang Christmas songs. Sometimes people gave them some food or something to drink.

People open gifts and eat delicious food on Christmas day. It is a tradition. But maybe the best part of Christmas is being with family and friends.

1   Understanding the Story

Answer the following questions.

1.   When is Christmas (give 2 answers)?

_____

2.   What do mothers tell their children to do before Christmas?

_____

3.   What do many Canadians eat around Christmas time?

_____

4.   Are many stores open on Christmas Day?

_____

5.   What do the words, 'or else' mean?

   a) also   b) if not   c) because of

2   Let's Practice...Verb + To + Verb

Verbs like *want, need,* and *hope* can be used with other verbs:
   * I <u>want to drink</u> some water.
   * I <u>need to fix</u> my car.
   * I <u>hope to watch</u> a movie tomorrow.

These verbs, called INFINITIVES, follow this rule: verb + to + verb.

   Here is a short list of other infinitive verbs:

   Decide, forget, expect, learn, hate, love, plan, would like, promise, try

Exercise 1: Use one of the verbs above to finish the sentences. Use the verbs only 1 time:

1.   I _____ to speak French when I was 6 years old.

2.   She _____ to visit Italy. It is her dream.

3.   He _____ to do his homework, so his teacher is upset.

4.   Many students _____ to write tests.

5.   I _____ my friend to meet her at Tokyo Station.

Exercise 2: Answer the questions below. Try to use complete sentences.

   1. What do you hate to do in the morning? _____

   2. What do you hope to do this weekend? _____

   3. What do you sometimes forget to do? _____

   4. When did you learn to drive? _____

   5. These days, what are you trying to do? _____

3   Writing: Holidays

With your partner or by yourself, write about what you (or your partner) do on special days.

1. Next Christmas, I want _____

2. Around January 01, I go to parties to _____

3. On Valentine's Day, I need to _____

4. On holidays, I sometimes promise my friends to _____

5. On holidays, I like to _____

6. On the next holiday, I would like to _____

7. On my birthday, I hope to _____

4   Sentence Order

Read the story about Christmas below, and put the sentences in the right order (1-9).

_____   He bought her a new vacuum because her old vacuum was...old.

_____   He wanted to buy his wife a present.

_____   She picked up the heavy box, and started to open her present.

__1__   One week before Christmas, Jack went shopping.

_____   She saw her present, and said, "Oh Jack, the box is sooooooo big. What is it?"

_____   On Christmas morning, Jack's wife looked under the Christmas tree.

_____   When she saw the vacuum, she got angry and tried to hit Jack with the vacuum.

_____   Jack smiled and said, "Open it up!"

_____   Jack decided to run away.

Unit 15
Winter Activities

Warm-up Questions

1. Can you skate or ski?

2. How often do you go fishing?

3. In winter, what do you never do?

4. Do people in your city do something special in winter?

5. What do people wear in winter?

VOCABULARY

Finish the sentences below using words from the vocabulary.

Activities, extremely, festivals, unusual, even, ponds, rinks, stove, thousands of, charity, carnivals

1. Small lakes are called _____.

2. It is hot this winter. That is _____.

3. I make food in a pot on my _____.

4. I like ice cream, _____ miso ice cream.

5. People donate money to _____ (s).

6. It is _____ cold in the Arctic.

Winter Activities

There are 4 seasons in Canada. In spring, flowers bloom and birds sing. In summer, the weather is hot and the days are long. In fall, leaves change colour and the wind starts to get cool. And in winter, snow falls and people try to stay warm. But winter can also be a very exciting time across Canada, and Canadians do many interesting activities.

Winter in Canada can be very long and extremely cold. January is the coldest month in almost all of Canada's big cities. The coldest city is Winnipeg (average -22.8C), and the warmest is Vancouver, BC (6.5C).

But Canadians don't just sit inside and stay warm in winter. They do many activities and have many festivals. Some of these activities are unusual. For example, some people like to go ice fishing, go dog sledding, or go swimming in freezing cold water. But usually, Canadians go skiing and go skating, even on very cold days.

In most parts of Canada, on frozen ponds or on outdoor rinks, Canadians like to go skating. In every town (町), there are free skating rinks outside. Some people even make skating rinks in their yards (庭).

Many people also go skiing in winter. One popular Canadian ski resort is Whistler, B.C. People can ski from November to August, and Whistler is the biggest ski resort in North America.

Some Canadians also go ice fishing in winter. On frozen lakes or rivers, fishermen sometimes build a small house on the ice. These houses can have a TV, stove, bathroom and even a shower.

Fishing in winter is cold, but swimming in winter is very, very cold. But that is what thousands of Canadians do every New Year's Day across Canada. In Oakville, Ontario, people go swimming in the icy cold water for charity.

Canada is a cold country in winter. But it doesn't mean that Canadians don't have fun. There are wine festivals in Nova Scotia, an ice hotel in Quebec City, and amazing carnivals across the whole country. But, if you go to Canada in the winter time, bring a warm jacket.

1 Understanding the Story

Answer the questions below from the story 'Winter Activities'.

1. Where do many Canadians skate?

   _____

2. Why is Whistler special?

   _____

3. Why do some Canadians go swimming in winter?

   _____

4. Where is the World Pond Hockey Championship?

   _____

2 Let's Practice...Using *GO*

We use GO + ING to talk about activities: go skiing, go fishing and go shopping.
For sports like baseball and tennis, we usually use the verb PLAY.

Exercise 1: Finish these sentences using the words from the list below. Use each word only

Mountain climbing, play, sight seeing, shopping, fishing, camping, running, see, skiing, dancing

1. Nobuko never eats seafood, so she never goes _____.

2. Yoko loves music, so sometimes she goes _____ with her friends.

3. Sumie loves to go _____ and buy many things.

4. Mount Fuji is beautiful. I want to go _____ there.

5. In summer, many people go _____. They make a fire, and sleep outside.

6. I want to run a marathon, so I must go _____ everyday.

7. When I traveled to Rome, I went _____ and saw fantastic places.

8. In winter, lots of people go _____ in places like Niseko or Whistler.

9. I feel sick. I will go to the hospital to _____ a doctor.

10. Masao and Yumiko went to the park to _____ tennis.

Here are more examples for using GO + ing. They are all activities.

Go biking	Go fishing	Go mountain climbing
Go bird watching	Go hunting	Go sailing
Go bowling	Go jogging	Go scuba diving
Go camping	Go skiing	Go shopping
Go dancing	Go swimming	Go skating

Exercise 2: Practice using GO + ing by completing the following sentences:

1.   I want to go _____ next year.

2.   On Sunday, I sometimes go downtown to _____.

3.   I have never gone _____ in my life.

4.   I don't like to go _____ because _____.

5.   When I go _____, I always have fun.

We can also use GO to talk about movements of place.

ヒント
- I will go home after class.
- I usually go to Nakajima Park in the morning.

NOTE: Work, bed, school, jail (刑務所), and church (教会) are a little special.
    If you do an action at those places, not just visiting, we say:

ヒント
- I go to bed at 10pm. (Not "go to a bed")
- My friend went to jail (he is a bad guy).
- You go to school every Monday. (You study)

Exercise 3: Answer the questions below using complete sentences.

1.   When do you go home?
    _____

2.   When do you usually go to bed (あなたは普段何時に寝ますか)?
    _____

3.   When do you go to work?
    _____

4.   Have you ever been in jail?
    _____

Unit 16
Multicultural Country

Warm-up Questions

1. How many foreign countries have you visited? Which was your favourite?

2. What is your favourite foreign food?

3. Should Japan allow more foreign people into the country?

4. Would you like to live in a multi-cultural (異質) country?

5. What kind of foreign products (外国製品) do you like?

Answer the questions below.

Permanently, move to, immigrants, overcrowded, miners, agreed, degrees, compared to

1. Which city would you like to move to in the world? _____

2. Compared to your teacher, who is older? _____

3. Are there too many foreigners in Japan? _____

4. Which places are overcrowded in your city? _____

Multicultural Country

Not many people from foreign countries live permanently in Japan. This is very different from Canada. People from around the world move to Canada and live in big cities like Vancouver, Toronto and Montreal.

About 175 000 immigrants (移民) move to Canada every year. Almost 20% of all people in Canada were born in another country.

Every year, a small number of Japanese people move to Canada. Vancouver is a popular place for Japanese people. Manzo Nagano was the first Japanese person to move to Vancouver in 1877. If he didn't go to Canada, maybe fewer Japanese people would live in Canada today.

By 1901, about 5 000 Japanese people immigrated (移住) to Canada. Many of them were young Japanese men. They came from poor farming or fishing villages like Hiroshima, Shiga, Wakayama and Kagoshima. They did not have luxurious lives.

At that time, these Japanese cities were overcrowded. If they wanted a job, it was hard to find one. When these men moved to Canada, a lot of them worked as fishermen, farmers, and miners. It was a hard life for them.

In the early 1900s, more Japanese women started to come to Canada. Some of them were 'picture brides'. The Japanese man only saw the woman's picture. The couple agreed to marry before they met.

These days, Japanese people moving to Canada are usually women. They have university degrees. If they marry, they don't often marry Japanese men. But the number of Japanese people moving to Canada is very low. Only .2% of Canadians are Japanese.

Compared to Canada, the number of foreigners in Japan is low. About 2.5 million foreigners live in Japan. Nearly half are from China and Korea. In 2010, the Asahi newspaper asked if Japanese people wanted to open Japan to more foreigners, and close to 65% said no.

1 Understanding the Story

Answer the questions below from the story 'Multi-Cultural Country'.

1.   How many Canadians are born outside of Canada?

_____

2.   Why is Manzo Nagano important in Canada?

_____

3.   What kinds of jobs did the first Japanese people in Canada have?

_____

4.   Why did Japanese men decide to move to Canada?

_____

2 Let's Practice...Using *IF*

There are 4 ways we can use IF. Note how the verbs are used:

1. The 'zero' conditional: Used for things that happen now or always.

    EXAMPLE: If I am hungry, I eat some food.

2. Type 1 conditional: Used for real situations that happen in the future.

    EXAMPLE: If it snows tomorrow, I will wear a hat.

3. Type 2 conditional: Used for unreal situations. They can happen now or any time.

    EXAMPLE: If I were a bird, I would fly to Hawaii.

4. Type 3 conditional: Used for past situations that did not happen. In other words, an unreal past that explains a probable result.

    EXAMPLE: If he had studied for the test, he would have passed.

Exercise 1: Answer the questions using complete sentences.

1. What do you do if you are tired?   _____

2. What do you do if you are angry?   _____

3. What are you going to do if it snows tomorrow? _____

4. What will you do if you are sick tomorrow morning? _____

5. If you found a bag of money, what would you do? _____

6. If you hadn't studied today, what would you have done? _____

Exercise 2: Circle the best answer to the questions below.

1. If people smoke, they
A) spend lots of money
B) will spend lots of money
C) would spend lots of money

2. If there is an earthquake in Tokyo, people
A) are hurt
B) will be hurt
C) would be hurt

3. If I am thirsty, I
A) drink water
B) will drink water
C) would drink water

4. If I met an alien, I
A) feel afraid
B) will feel afraid
C) would feel afraid

3   Discussion Topics

With a partner, discuss the following questions. Be ready to answer them in class.

1. If you went to Prince Edward Island (P.E.I.), what would you bring? _____

2. If you saw a polar bear in your house what would you do? _____

3. If you have no money, what do you do? _____

4. If you moved to Canada, where would you like to live? _____

5. If you visit a temple, what do you do? _____

Answer Key

Unit 1 Anne of Green Gables

Vocabulary - 1. translated   2. orphan   3. published   4. survive   5. charm

Part 2 - 1. B   2. A   3. C   4. B   5. B

Part 3 - 1. enjoys   2. own   3. survive   4. return   5. keep   6. taught   7. met (or saw)   8. will translate   9. help   10. grew up   11. tried   12. saw   13. decided   14. became   15. die

Part 4 Step 1 - Can you HEAR a horse RUNNING through a gentle hill   A horse carriage IS COMING towards us   They are coming to SEE us   They must BE coming to see us   Somebody IS TAKING me to the avenue of white flowers   Hometown of the wind   They are TAKING me   They ARE taking me
Step 2 Past Tense verbs - Come/CAME   Hear/HEARD   Run/RAN   See/SAW   Take/TOOK   Burn/BURNT or BURNED   Be/WAS or WERE

Unit 2 Bears in Canada

Vocabulary - 1. afraid of   2. weigh   3. full of   4. attack   5. female

Part 1 - 1. B   2. B   3. A (over 2.7 meters tall)   4. B   5. A

Unit 3 The Arctic

Vocabulary - 1. arctic fox   2. igloo   3. frozen   4. melts   5. seal

Part 1 - 1. False   2. True   3. False   4. False   5. True

Part 3 - 1. The man on the left is heavier than the man on the right   2. The boy is younger than the girl.   3. The man on the left is more handsome   4. The woman is angrier than the man.

Part 4 - 1. What is the coldest city in Japan?   2. What is the largest country in the world?   3. What is the most interesting TV show in Japan?   4. Who is taller than you in this class?   5. What is the most expensive city in the world?

Unit 4 Canada's Only Desert

Vocabulary - 1. cactus   2. owl   3. rattlesnake   4. temperature   5. ride his horse

Part 1 - Desert, close to, In, plants, owl, under, horses, grapes

Part 3 - 1. on   2. in   3. up   4. near (between)   5. under   6. near (behind)   7. in   8. past (outside)   9. across   10. beside
Part 4 - #2 Yuki went to an airport, and got on a plane. #3 When she arrived in Canada, she was surprised. #4 There was a lot of snow on the ground, but Yuki didn't like snow. #5 Yuki was cold, so she asked a man, "Where is a warm place in Canada?" #6 The man answered, "You should go to the Osoyoos Desert by bus." #7 So, Yuki got on a bus, and went to the desert. #8 First, Yuki went to a hotel in the desert. Next, she looked around the city. #9 Osoyoos City was very beautiful, with nice buildings and warm weather. #10 She had lots of fun on her trip.

Unit 5 Canada's van Gogh

Part 3 Exercise II - There are many possible answers for these sentences. Here are some of these answers.

1. much / a lot of / enough   2. enough   3. many   4. much   5. a few   6. little / hardly any   7. much / a lot of / plenty of   8. few   9. many   10. much

Unit 6 Money

Vocabulary - collect, hobby, nobody, antique, bills, valuable, quit

Part 3 - 1. How many people live in your hometown?   2. How tall are you?   3. How much water do you drink everyday?   4. How big is your bed?   5. Do you like steak? How about hamburgers?   6. How much does your watch cost?   7. How did you come here today?   8. How far is your home from here?

Unit 7 Religion

Vocabulary - 1. outside   2. servant   3. Homeless   4. meditate   5. Greedy

Part 3 - 1. told   2. said   3. spoke   4. spoke (or speaks)   5. asked   6. asked   7. told (or asked)   8. asked 9. speak   10. say

Part 4 - Buddhist monks wake up early every morning in Chuo Ji. This is a place where monks train. There are about 15 monks who live there. It is a big building with many rooms, a few statues, and a lot of flowers. The leader of Chuo Ji is a very wise man. He teaches other monks how to be good. Being a monk is an important job. I respect monks, and I really like their hair style.

Unit 8 Halifax Explosion

Vocabulary - 1. each other   2. port   3. explosion   4. shore   5. hit

Part 2 Exercise 1 - 1. There are   2. There is   3. It   4. are   5. are   6. It   7. There is / it is   8. It is   9. there is   10. It is <u>Monday</u>   11. It is <u>about 5 minutes</u>   12. It is <u>cold</u>
Exercise 2 - 1. There are many books in the bag   2. There is a lot of (or LOTS OF) money in the big, brown bag 3. There is a letter on the table for my mom   4. He told me (or SAID TO ME) that it was 2 o'clock (or 2 pm)   5. It is a sunny day today, so let's go outside

Unit 9 The Titanic

Vocabulary - 1. tried to   2. coward   3. sank   4. sailor / skilled at   5. luxurious

Part 2 Exercise 1 - 1. C   2. A   3. B
Exercise 2 (there are many possible answers) - 1. shouldn't   2. can't   3. didn't   4. couldn't   5. won't   6. aren't   7. don't   8. isn't   9. don't   10. don't / won't

Part 3 (there are many possible answers) - Yesterday I drove my car. I am a good driver, but I had an accident. My car crashed into a truck. I hurt my neck. I needed to meet a doctor. I went to a hospital. I met a doctor. He said I was not hurt. My car is destroyed. So, I took a taxi home.

Unit 10 Japanese People in Canada

Part 2 Exercise 1 - 1. money   2. tea   3. bed   4. trouble   5. phone call   6. friends   7. plan   8. happy   9. study   10. mistake
Exercise 2 - 1. in   2. by   3. of   4. with   5. from

Part 3 - 1. How do you make your wife happy?   2. How often do you make your bed?   3. What plan did you make this year?   4. How much money do you make?   5. What makes you angry?

Unit 11 Newfoundland

Vocabulary - 1. float   2. skunk   3. cricket   4. moose   5. seal

Part 2 Exercise 1 - 1. need   2. understand   3. looks like   4. surprise   5. know   6. belongs   7. hear   8. agree   9. promised   10. wish

Unit 12 Winnie the Pooh

Vocabulary - 1. donated   2. take care of   3. adventures   4. a wood   5. at that time   6. called it

Part 2 - 1. met   2. bought   3. came / (time)   4. took / (place)   5. was   6. wrote / (person or people)   7. did / (place or time)   8. went / (i.e. week)   9. sold   10. got / made

Part 3 - Last year, Yoko took a trip to Vancouver, Canada. She had a very fun time. She went with her friend Shinzo. They saw many beautiful things, ate delicious food, and bought many souvenirs. They drove to Mount Manzo Nagano, and met other Japanese tourists there. Yoko walked into a forest because she saw a baby bear. Then she saw the bear's mother, a grizzly bear. Shinzo hit the grizzly bear with his shoe, and the 2 bears ran away. Yoko was lucky. Shinzo was a hero.

Unit 13 Remembrance Day

Vocabulary - 1. soldier   2. dangerous   3. protect   4. silent   5. conflict

Part 2 - 1. In the past   2. right now   3. In the future   4. soon   5. ___ days ago   6. These days   7. Every winter (or every year)   8. In 1964

Part 3 - 1 Buddhism comes to Japan   2 Shoguns rule Japan   3 General Perry forces Japan to trade   4 Emperor Meiji makes Japan a powerful and rich country   5 The Great Kanto earthquake destroys Tokyo and Yokohama   6 Yukawa Hideki is the first Japanese to win the Nobel Prize in physics   7 The Summer Olympics are in Tokyo for the first time 8 John Lennon and Yoko Ono get married   9 Okinawa is returned to Japan

Unit 14 Wish You a Merry Christmas

Part 2 Exercise I - 1. learned   2. would like   3. forgot   4. hate   5. promised

Part 4 - 1 One week before Christmas, Jack went shopping   2 He wanted to buy his wife a present   3 He bought her a new vacuum because her old vacuum was...old   4 On Christmas morning, Jack's wife woke up early, and looked under the Christmas tree   5 She saw her present, and said, "Oh Jack, the box is sooooooo big. What is it?"   6 Jack smiled and said, "Open it up!"   7 She picked up the heavy box, and started to open her present   8 When she saw the vacuum, she got angry and tried to hit Jack with the vacuum   9 Jack decided to run away.

Unit 15 Winter Activities

Vocabulary - 1. ponds 2. unusual   3. stove   4. even   5. charity   6. extremely
Part 2 Exercise I - 1. fishing   2. dancing   3. shopping   4. mountain climbing   5. camping   6. running   7. sight seeing   8. skiing   9. see   10. play

Unit 16 Multi Cultural Country

Part 2 Exercise 2 - 1. A   2. B   3. A   4. C

CONNECTING
CULTURES

Toem
Publishing